Original title:
The Locket's Story

Copyright © 2025 Creative Arts Management OÜ
All rights reserved.

Author: Tobias Sterling
ISBN HARDBACK: 978-1-80586-217-8
ISBN PAPERBACK: 978-1-80586-689-3

The Pendant's Silent Confessions

Once swung from a neck, so bold and bright,
It whispered of secrets, tucked in the night.
A dog once mistook it, thought it a treat,
Chasing the sparkle, he tripped on his feet.

In a drawer it now lies, a treasure unseen,
With tales of a love that just might have been.
It giggles at moments, the laughs, and the tears,
Reminding its owner of those silly years.

Unveiling the Heart's Secrets

A heart-shaped charm with a twist of fate,
Caught in the riddle of a date too late.
It trembles with tales of awkward first dates,
Where spilled drinks and stumbles became our traits.

It held a promise from junior prom night,
But the dance was a checklist of awkward delight.
With every swing, it spins stories anew,
Of all the mishaps that just might ring true.

A Journey Through Glass and Gold

Around a neck it sparkled, a vision of flair,
Yet sometimes it tangled in a way that's unfair.
A cat gave a leap, thinking it a toy,
Leaving behind chaos, not one moment of joy.

In parties it danced, a diva in style,
Accidentally caught in a napkin's vile smile.
Tales wrapped in laughter, shared over drinks,
Finding such joy in the mischief it links.

Nostalgia Caught in a Glimpse

From a box in the attic, it shines with a grin,
With memories trapped where all stories begin.
It giggles at fashion trends long gone and stale,
Like bell-bottoms and platforms that surely prevail.

Behind dusty glass, it holds silent cheers,
Of late-night adventures and questionable peers.
With every glance back, time takes on a twist,
Laughing at moments you simply can't miss.

A Glimpse of Yesterday's Love

In a dusty drawer, a heart did hide,
With quirky charms and a story wide.
Each glance reveals a kiss gone wrong,
But oh, how the laughter makes us strong!

A picture of love in a tiny frame,
With mismatched socks, oh what a shame!
A giggle erupts, memories collide,
As we trip down memory's silly slide.

Fragments of an Untold Tale

Once a token forged from mischief's heat,
Worn by a clown with two left feet.
Each twist and turn, a spiral dance,
In the circus of love, we took a chance.

A glance at that charm sparks a grin,
Did we really think we'd ever win?
The punchlines echo, faint yet clear,
Of a romance that tickled the ear.

Charm of the Hidden Past

Nestled inside a tangled mess,
A pendant of joy, a charm of stress.
A love note scribbled with ink so blue,
Said, "You're odd, but I still love you!"

A whisper of laughter from yesteryear,
As we chase the gnomes that hop with cheer.
Remnants of a treasure, silly and bright,
Each jingle we share is pure delight.

Memories Anchored in Metal

An anchor dipped in a sea of glee,
Kept tales of chaos, just you and me.
With every glance, a giggle erupts,
Recalling our antics, smiles are corrupt.

Ringlets of laughter, a sparkle's embrace,
Moments of madness, life's funny race.
Each twisty trinket tells stories so grand,
Of love's crazy journey, hand in hand.

Charmed Secrets and Gentle Reminders

In a box made of brass, lies a trinket so bright,
It holds all my secrets, from morning 'til night.
A small charm of laughter, on days full of gloom,
It wiggles and giggles, bringing joy to my room.

With each tiny jingle, it dances with glee,
Reciting my stories, like a tongue-in-cheek spree.
Its smiley facade, oh so cheeky and wild,
Is the keeper of fun, a mischievous child.

Soulful Adornments of Memory

In the depths of my drawer, there lies quite a gem,
A whisper of tales, each one worth ahem!
With smiles and mishaps captured within,
It giggles at mishaps with a cheeky grin.

Plastic pearls and glitter, oh the glamour it brings,
While recalling my crushes and all of their flings.
It chuckles at love notes, so cringy yet dear,
Reminding me hilariously of yesteryear.

Lost and Found in Precious Metal

A ring that went missing, oh where could it flee?
Did it roll down the couch, or escape to a tree?
With a clink and a flutter, it finally appeared,
Laughing at mishaps, it's oddly endeared.

It tells tales of socks that have vanished from view,
And all the odd moments, both silly and true.
With shine in its laugh, it glares with delight,
For the stories it holds, make everything right!

Inscriptions of What Was

Upon a small plate, there are scribbles of laughter,
Of flirty moments, and silly chatter.
A dance of nostalgia, it sways to the beat,
A plate full of mischief, oh what a treat!

The etchings hold whispers of crushes long gone,
With doodles of kittens that played 'til the dawn.
Each scratch tells a chuckle, a giggle or two,
A treasure of whimsy, in metals so true.

Glimmers of Lost Time

In a box where memories hide,
A key to laughter, just inside.
It tickled thoughts of days gone by,
With chuckles shared and silly sighs.

A photograph with a bad haircut,
Makes me laugh, oh what a nut!
Each smile sparkles, shines so bright,
Like disco balls in fading light.

A dance of dorky, silly moves,
Remembered joy, it always grooves.
Glimpses of chaos, sweet and wild,
Leaving me grinning like a child.

So here's to those moments we miss,
Each memory's a little bliss.
In that box, I'll keep it neat,
Glimmers of joy, laughter's sweet treat.

Beneath the Surface of Sentiment

In the treasure chest of my heart,
Sentiments dance, a quirky art.
Each one wriggles like a fish,
Beneath the waves, they swish and swish.

A note from ages, written in haste,
With doodles and hearts, such a funny taste.
It giggles, it chuckles, oh what a find,
Tickling the corners of my mind.

The socks I lost, they tell a tale,
Of mismatched nights and sneaky trails.
Beneath the surface, whimsy plays,
In the depths of my heart, endless rays.

So let's dive deep, let's have some fun,
In the sea of laughter, we can run.
Sentiment swims, floats like a breeze,
Tickling the heart with joyful ease.

A Tapestry of Tender Moments

Weaving threads of laughter's praise,
Through moments sweet, a funny daze.
Each stitch a giggle, a wink, a tease,
In the tapestry, our hearts find ease.

A splatter of paint, it went awry,
On the wall, a rainbowed sky.
With every mess, a story spins,
Bringing forth all our little wins.

The comical fits when we were teens,
Chasing dreams in silly scenes.
Stitches of madness, colors bright,
Chuckles echo in the soft twilight.

So cherish this canvas, wild and free,
A tapestry where we laugh with glee.
Memories linger like threads of gold,
In this quilt, our fun moments unfold.

The Weight of Yesterday's Wishes

A box of dreams from days of yore,
Wishes wrapped in laughter's core.
Each one giggles, with a nudge,
As if to tease, "Quit being a grudge!"

The rubber chicken, once adored,
Holds echoes of laughter, never bored.
Its silly squawk, it reignites,
Good times shared in wild delights.

A half-eaten cake, a party gone strange,
With icing faces all out of range.
Every slice hides a playful whim,
Wrapped up in smiles, never dim.

So load the box with joyful cheer,
For every wish that draws us near.
We'll yank out yesterday, in a playful quest,
Light as a feather, our hearts feel blessed.

The Dance of Forgotten Affections

In a drawer, a heart does sway,
With memories tucked so far away.
It twirls to tunes of yesteryear,
While dust bunnies cheer with a hearty cheer.

Old photos fumble, a photo bomb,
Two lovers caught in a silly calm.
With joyful laughs that never age,
They dance to love's own silly stage.

The fabric whispers, soft and slight,
Threading tales of day and night.
As giggles echo in empty halls,
Past romances trip and fall.

Each clasp a giggle, each chain a jest,
In this memory chest, they take their rest.
With every clasp a chuckle unfurls,
In forgotten affection, love still whirls.

Thread of Time and Sentiment

A string of days, both tight and loose,
Wrapped in tales where laughter's no excuse.
Each knot a giggle, each loop a cheer,
Time weaves memories we hold dear.

Worn-out stickers from days of lore,
Adventures chased, but never bore.
A paper heart that's slightly bent,
Holds the gags we never meant.

A thread unravels, a laugh flies high,
As mishaps spin through days gone by.
Each pull a memory, every tug a laugh,
In the quilt of life, we find our path.

Yet stitching seams might come undone,
With mismatched colors, oh what fun!
Through fraying edges, smiles emerge,
In the chaos, we find our urge.

A Keepsake's Silent Oath

A trinket sparkles, faint yet bold,
Beneath the silver, stories unfold.
With every twist and turn it takes,
A promise lingers, even when it shakes.

Inside the clasp, a pieced-up tale,
Of birthday cakes and dreaded mail.
With candy wrappers in disarray,
And notes of love that went astray.

It whispers secrets in the quiet night,
Where giggles bridge the dark with light.
A ring's fierce bond may seem so grand,
But it's laughter that joins hand in hand.

So here we stand with tales to weave,
In a tapestry of joy and grieve.
With heartfelt jests, we keep afloat,
For in this silence, the heart will gloat.

Reflections on a Shimmering Surface

In a puddle, reflections dance,
Echoes of love and a glance.
With ripples tickling the inner cheek,
Each splash a laugh, both bold and meek.

An old mirror, cracked yet true,
Shows the mischief of me and you.
With goofy faces and silly grins,
In the blur of ages, joy begins.

We chase our shadows, race the sun,
Tickling time till the day is done.
Through shifting shapes, we share our glee,
In this merry twist, we find the key.

So let the past reflect with cheer,
In each gleaming glance, the heart we steer.
For every shimmer hides a tale,
Of laughter, love, on life's great scale.

Chasing Shadows of the Heart

In a drawer, it found a seat,
Where old socks and dust bunnies meet.
It giggled at memories, quite absurd,
Of love notes and snickers, all unheard.

A glittering gem, a tale to tell,
Of hearts that once danced, oh so well.
It whispers of secrets, that sometimes stung,
Like passages sung by a tongue that's sprung.

With a nudge, it pokes at the old shoes,
Reciting old romances and silly clues.
"Remember that time you tripped on air?
Your folks thought it funny; you had no care!"

So here it sits, with a chuckle and sigh,
A keeper of follies, oh my, oh my!
This shine holds the stories that time can't erase,
With moments so quirky, they can't lose face.

Love's Timeless Embrace

Nestled in velvet, it starts to grin,
Recalling the laughter, the silly din.
Two lovesick birds, on a comedic spree,
With puns thrown like petals, wild and free.

It remembers the date when hearts first zoomed,
Under awkward glances, both feeling doomed.
"Did you just wink or blink at my snack?
If this love's a race, we've both lost track!"

Oh, the slips, the trips, and the ice cream spills,
All wrapped in sweetness with definite thrills.
A sprinkle of humor takes center stage,
As they dance on the lines of a comical page.

In a pocket it waits, for the next silly day,
To sing of their antics in its own special way.
With laughter its currency, it surely can stake,
For love always flourishes in moments we make!

The Memory Enshrined

Once worn by a lover, quite flustered and shy,
It holds every giggle, each whispering why.
With tales of the past, it chuckles and beams,
Like a cat with nine lives and wild, crazy dreams.

Each scratch and each dent tells a story or two,
Of the time they both hid from a flying shoe.
Serenading the phone calls that went slightly wrong,
Loud singing in showers, a whimsical song.

At times it's a lens, for a sitcom on cue,
The mishaps of love just seem to pursue.
Every heart tug, every cranky old joke,
It rolls in delight, like a playful poke.

So here it remains, ever bright, fully kind,
With laughter ensconced in the love that it's lined.
For nestled in laughter, the heart finds its tune,
A melody merry, like the sun and the moon.

Forgotten Whispers of Affection

In a shadowy nook, it guards a grin,
Of romance gone rogue, where giggles begin.
Each whisper it hoards, a tale from the past,
Of how love can stumble, yet still, ever last.

"Remember the time you danced on the floor?
Tripped over your feet, then you begged for more?"
With laughter painted, the days carry on,
This shiny old keeper, forever a con.

It peeks through the cracks, of each joyful shout,
While side-eyeing memories, without a doubt.
A wink and a smile, it bestows in delight,
For love's best moments are crafted at night.

Now tucked away, with a dust-bunny friend,
It cackles alive; will the fun ever end?
In quirky old tales, they find what they seek,
With laughs that echo, so sweet and unique.

Glimpses of a Cherished Past

Once lost in a drawer, gold glinted with glee,
A treasure of memories, where could it be?
Dust bunnies were plotting, they laughed and they mocked,
"Find me if you can!" said the locket that clocked.

One day it appeared, but upside-down,
Hiding with socks, oh what a clown!
It rattled and chuckled, "Hey, not so fast!"
Each twist of fate, a hilarious blast.

It whispered old secrets of love gone awry,
With cheeky little tales that made passersby sigh.
The puppy love story, a prance and a spin,
Made everyone giggle, including a grin.

So here it remains, full of quirks and delight,
A locket that laughs through the day and the night.
With a sparkle of history, oh what a blend,
Of humor and warmth from a jewel and a friend.

The Allure of a Forgotten Token

In a drawer of dreams, an odd thing I found,
A curious charm with a story profound.
It matched with odd socks and a broken old shoe,
Whispering tales of adventures anew.

"Once I was shiny!" it clanged with joy,
Echoing laughter like a playful toy.
With memories tangled like a plate of spaghetti,
It made me ponder—was my love ever ready?

The days of our youth, were silly and bright,
Chasing after moths in the cool summer night.
This charm with its wisdom only giggles and grins,
Took me back to moments where laughter begins.

Now displayed on a shelf, it winks with delight,
As if to say, "Look, I've been quite the sight!"
A trinket of fun from a time long ago,
Spinning stories around like a carnival show.

A Covenant of Heart and Time

In a pocket so deep, I found two old keys,
They jingled and jangled and danced in the breeze.
"Unlock the past!" they chirped with a laugh,
A promise of joy, my own little staff.

I turned them with glee, but they led me to socks,
A treasure of laundry, a wardrobe paradox.
Amongst all the chaos, a smile popped free,
"Who knew love lived here?" said the keys with glee.

Poking through memories, names that could rhyme,
Moments that tickled the edges of time.
And there on the floor, beneath all the dust,
Came a dance of the heart, an overdue bust.

Together these charms weave a tapestry bright,
Of laughter and love, of loss and delight.
A comical twist, in this journey we roam,
With keys and wild socks, I laugh all the way home.

Shadows of Love Encircled

A picture inside, oh what could it be?
Two faces entwined, are they smiling at me?
With shadows and giggles, the memory spun,
Whispers of mischief, oh what a fun run!

Each frame tells a story, a mix-up of sorts,
Where love was a game played in various courts.
A wink here, a nudge there, oh what a show,
Time traveled in laughter with each little glow.

Thus captured in metal, the mischief does leak,
With jokes and sweet antics, that make my heart squeak.
From pranks of the past to the shenanigans planned,
This charm holds the echoes of moments so grand.

It sways on my neck, like a jester, it prances,
Reminding of love in all its funny dances.
So here's to the past, where hilarity gleams,
In shadows of love, forever it beams.

Reflections in a Gilded Frame

In a frame that's shiny and bright,
There lives a tale of pure delight.
It's not a gem, but sadly a hair,
From that dog who would never share.

A dance of dust in the sun's warm rays,
It sparkles and shines in so many ways.
But every glance leads to a sneer,
That hair looks like it's been aged a year!

With each new story, the laughter grows,
It's more than a hair; it's a funny nose!
A poodle pranced, and there it stayed,
A legacy of fur that won't soon fade.

So here's to the laughter, we raise a toast,
To silly things that we love the most.
Some memories lock up all the fun,
In a picture that's sillier than anyone!

A Love Held Close

Nestled 'round my neck, it sits tight,
A heart-shaped charm, oh what a sight!
It jingles and jangles, oh what a sound,
With every move, it's spinning around.

This love I wear, it's quite a gem,
Though moths might take a bit of a swim.
A threadbare ribbon, tattered and worn,
It's been through battles, it surely has sworn!

The neighbors all stare with laughter and cheer,
At the mishap of wearing my love so near.
But every strap and awkward twist,
Holds moments of joy that can't be missed.

Let laughter be shared, like a treasure box,
In this silly heart, my love awkwardly rocks.
So I'll wear this charm, though it may seem odd,
For love isn't perfect, it's just a little flawed!

Shadows of Enchantment

In twilight's glow, a shadow plays,
A whimsical tale of silly ways.
Two goofy gnomes in a dance-off beat,
While squirrels cheer from their leafy seat.

Their hats too big and shoes too small,
They trip and tumble, giving it all.
With every fall, I'm doubled in glee,
Oh what a sight—this shadowy spree!

Under the moon, they spin and sway,
Creating laughter in their own funny way.
A shimmery shadow that glows at night,
It whispers secrets with pure delight.

So whenever you stumble, just look around,
For shadows might lead to the joy that's found.
Life's little quirks are the best part of fate,
Embrace the shadows; don't sit and wait!

The Story Beneath the Surface

Beneath my shirt, a mystery lies,
A secret told in hopeful sighs.
A button missing, a thread that's loose,
It dangles and wiggles like a silly moose!

I've worn this shirt through thick and thin,
Its tales of spills and where I've been.
Ketchup stains and a coffee blot,
Each mark a laugh; why fret a lot?

It holds the memories of things I've spilled,
From odd little moments I never instilled.
A pocket's treasure, a gum wrapper muse,
Documents of joy, oh what can I use?

So here's to the fabric that wraps me tight,
With laughter stitched in every bite.
Life's woven stories may fray and bend,
But the heart stays true, on that you can depend!

The Unveiling of Affection

A tiny trinket, full of charm,
It swung around my neck, cause no harm.
Inside it holds a scrap of yarn,
A cat's old toy, oh what a disarm!

I thought it precious, a love to share,
But now it's just a hairpin's lair.
My grandma giggled, with a knowing glare,
At memories trapped in thin, metal air.

Each glance reveals a secret delight,
That time's twisted tales bring forth at night.
Though not a diamond shining bright,
It's laughter's echo that feels just right.

Echoes of a Love Once Worn

A picture tucked in crinkled folds,
Of love so young, and daring bold.
It's faded fast, but does not scold,
   Instead it dances, a tale retold.

"Oh look," I chuckle, "what a sight!"
In goofy poses, we twirled with might.
I mime our moves, it feels so light,
That love, in jest, was pure delight.

My heart recalls those silly days,
Where laughter wiggled, in hair's wild ways.
Nostalgic whispers creep in, it stays,
Each moment cherished, through life's silly maze.

The Weight of What We Keep

A bauble shiny, nothing grand,
Yet it speaks volumes, more than planned.
Within it lies a crumb of sand,
From beach days long, a memory's brand.

What do we save? What brings us glee?
An old gum wrapper, a lost car key?
As laughter bubbles like a bright sea,
It's these tiny things that tell our spree.

Beneath the weight of all we hoard,
Are whispers of life in each memory stored.
Though mundane items might feel ignored,
They shape our battles, and joys adored.

Nostalgia in a Shining Embrace

In sunlight's grasp, a glimmer glows,
It twirls and bounces, then freely flows.
An anchor of fun from long ago,
Where giggles hid, and mischief shows.

Oh dear, what treasures my heart does keep,
From rubber ducks to doll's last leap.
Each laugh we shared is a mountain steep,
My fondest dreams in a box so deep.

An old string tied with a lopsided bow,
It weaves a tale of the silly and slow.
In laughter's light, our memories glow,
Nostalgia sings, with a cheeky flow.

Reflections of an Unwritten Romance

In a drawer, so dusty and deep,
A treasure waits while I snooze and sleep.
With images blurred and stories untold,
It chuckles at memories, both silly and bold.

A sigh for each glance, a wink for each sigh,
That old thing just sits there, oh my, oh my!
A heart tried to soar, but tripped on a shoe,
And laughter erupts like it always will do.

Why can't I find a key for this door?
It must be stuck with a love I adore.
While Cupid takes breaks, in his clumsy ballet,
My heart plays hide-and-seek, then laughs all the way.

So here's to the secrets inside that small box,
Whispers of crushes and fears, and odd socks.
A relic of giggles, where romance lies flat,
Holding all my stories, and a cat.

Radiance of Unseen Love

There's a charm nestled snug in my bag,
Each glance leaves me smiling, but it's a drag.
The sparkle it holds, I can hardly recall,
Like a dance with two left feet at the mall.

With each secret peek, it gives me a grin,
Did you see that? Oh, what a spin!
It plays hide-and-seek with my heart and my socks,
Giggling behind doors, and ticking like clocks.

A laugh escapes when I flip through it fast,
Remembering dates I'd rather forget last.
The shine of a crush who forgot my name,
Now hidden away, for my never-claimed fame.

Oh, the love that never was, quite a ride,
A twisty adventure with nowhere to hide.
Yet the heart finds joy in the silly and sweet,
Creating a glow beneath life's funny beat.

Sickles of Time and Tenderness

In the cupboard, there's a quirky tale,
A necklace, a laugh, and a heart that can fail.
With every tick of the clock, it reclines,
Waiting for moments like sips of fine wines.

Time stole the giggles, where did they go?
Oh, this fickle affair, what a peculiar show!
In the cornfield of love, we missed the harvest,
As my heart trips over each goofy jest.

From whispers at dawn to wild midday blush,
Moments entwined in a comical rush.
A dance through the backyard gave way to a spin,
And laughter erupts, let the antics begin!

With each secret tucked in a little heart beat,
There's a stack of old joys that make life complete.
Banter and banter, we ran 'round the bend,
In a romance unwritten, but filled with good friends.

Inscriptions of a Quiet Past

Dusted off memories linger in time,
Where laughter once echoed, and danced in their prime.
With secrets shyly tucked in a box,
Awkward love notes and mismatched socks.

What a compendium of giggles and sighs,
Like elephants tiptoeing with starlit skies.
A moment of glory, a slip, and a fall,
With each blushing glance, we laughed through it all.

I read the old lines—such terrible rhymes,
Each scribble illuminates spectacular crimes.
Where whimsy collides with the foolish and bright,
Creating a love story, absurd but just right.

Now the echoes have faded, but why let them rest?
With a chortle, I cherish the quirks and the jest.
Each twist of the past adds a smile to my day,
In the scrapbook of hearts, where laughter will stay.

Ties of the Heart's Journey

In a box, a trinket tight,
With whispers of love, oh what a sight!
When opened wide, it spills out cheer,
And laughs of memories echo near.

It twirled on a chain, once in a dance,
Caught in the grip of a fleeting chance.
A heart-shaped charm, with a wink and a grin,
Promised kisses from where it had been.

In grandma's purse, it caused a stir,
When she pulled it out, oh did we concur!
"Is that an amulet or snack?" we'd tease,
But she just smiled, playing the tease.

With tales from afar, it never gets old,
From earnest confessions to mere jokes told.
This heart enshrined, in a laughter spree,
Holds every giggle, and every "yippee!"

A Glimpse of Love's Echo

Caught in a pocket, it jangles and pops,
A tale of a crush and all the heart stops.
A photo that's faded but sprightly in hue,
Reminds us of what silly love can accrue.

"Hold tight!" we say, as our hearts do race,
The charm gets jealous of the smiles we face.
Tickling the fancies, it jumps in delight,
A relic that giggles, both day and night.

With a wink at the camera, it loves to pose,
Each glance and each chuckle, where affection grows.
"Oh dear heart," it chimes, "You wear me so well,
Let's spread joy like popcorn, in this spacious shell!"

So here's to the laughter, and love like a game,
An echo that whispers, how sweet isn't fame?
With each playful episode, let's clink and cheer,
For the joy of the heart is what draws you near!

The Timekeeper's Heart

A pocket timepiece of whimsical grace,
Reminds of love's dance, in a curious place.
Ticking away, with secrets it keeps,
It giggles and winks while the nostalgia creeps.

With each little tick, comes a story anew,
Of stolen glances and moments so true.
"Don't lose me now," it chimed with a jest,
For love's such a treasure, it knows it the best.

Clocks may be cruel, as they tell you to wait,
But this heart sings, "Oh, love won't be late!"
Through years of silliness captured in gold,
Each chuckle and giggle, a memory told.

So here's to the moments, blurred like a dream,
Where laughter composes love's most joyful theme.
Tick, tock, and giggle, let the heart play its part,
For time only gilds the bright flutters of heart.

Threads of Silver and Story

Threaded with tales, oh what a find!
Silver and glimmer that tickle the mind.
Each twist and turn, a laugh to unfold,
In the fabric of life, let the colors be bold.

Stitched in a whisper of playful delight,
A tapestry woven of day and of night.
With love that unravels each silly mistrust,
These knots tell of humor, in memories' rust.

As it dances and shimmies in pockets so deep,
It echoes enchantments, where secrets seep.
With giggles and banter, it twirls round the room,
A thread of enchantment that chases the gloom.

So let's weave together this playful embrace,
For each thread contains a smile we can trace.
With hearts intertwined, and laughter to share,
The stories we gather are beyond all compare!

Glimmering Threads of Sentiment

Once a trinket, shiny and bright,
Fell from a pocket, oh what a sight!
Chased by a dog, it rolled with glee,
Now it's a treasure for all to see.

In a corner, it found a new home,
Hiding from dust, it began to roam.
Threading through laughter and silly pranks,
This little piece sure called for thanks!

A tale of love wrapped in a twist,
It played hide and seek, and then it kissed.
With each little scratch, a story to tell,
Of parties, of giggles, and silly spells!

With glue and glitter, it's dressed anew,
A party of memories, all askew.
So here's to the laughter, the giggles and fun,
This bauble, this charm, oh how it won!

A Memento's Heartfelt Tale

Once lived a charm with flair so grand,
It danced on a shelf, wild and unplanned.
Tickled by dust, it whispered and grinned,
'Oh, what a time; let the fun begin!'

It played chess with a sock and a shoe,
Telling stories no one ever knew.
A burst of laughter when found in a stew,
This memento's tales just grew and grew!

In the depths of a drawer, it toasted toast,
To the days of the past, it loved the most.
With a wink and a wave, it skipped to the floor,
Who knew a trinket could be such a bore?

Lost in the attic, it found some old hats,
Dressed up as a king amongst dust bunnies and rats.
From paper to plastic, its fame spread wide,
A chuckle, a giggle, on this joyride!

Diary of a Forgotten Token

Turned dusty and old in a box on the shelf,
This token once danced with the light of itself.
Now it giggles at semi-forgotten days,
Bantering softly in whimsical ways.

A heart-shaped charm with a smirk and a wink,
Wants to remind us, take time to think.
About all the blunders we tend to ignore,
This diary of laughs always begs for more.

Found in a sandwich—what a surprise!
Stories it holds could light up the skies.
From mishaps to chuckles, it holds such a flair,
Each tale turns out to be quite the affair!

So here stands this wonder, a laugh and a tease,
It whispers sweet nothings with utmost ease.
For what is a token, but a wink of the past?
A chance to revisit the fun that won't last!

The Chain of Memories Unfurled

A chain of laughter, oh what a sight,
Link by link, it dances at night.
With a jingle and wiggle, it sparkles and shines,
Each memory's wacky, entwined like lines!

Oh, the circus it wore in a birthday hat,
Once flew on a kite, then landed with a splat.
A slide down the hill? What a mishap, indeed!
This crazy chain has a fun-loving creed!

From the kitchen's chaos to bedroom's charm,
It recalls with gusto, it brings such calm.
With each swirling tale, from silly to grand,
This chain of memories takes a stand!

So let's raise a cheer for this jolly old friend,
Through laughter and mayhem, may the fun never end.
For each little link holds a spark of delight,
A chain full of giggles, oh what a sight!

Shadows Dressed in Gold

In a drawer, secrets dance,
A shiny trinket, lost its chance.
Once a treasure, now a joke,
Whispers giggle, dreams revoke.

It once held love, now laughs on shelf,
It's smudged with dust, just like myself.
Hiding stories of silly blunders,
Golden trinkets, oh how it wonders!

It smiles at me with tarnished pride,
Where faded memories like to hide.
A heart's old promise, now a tease,
Tickling my heart like a playful breeze.

Oh, to remember, what could have been,
If only that charm could learn to grin!
With every glance, it winks in jest,
In its quiet charms, I find my rest.

Carvings from the Heart's Chamber

In wood and stone, laughter carved,
Little hearts, whimsically starved.
Each edge a giggle, each curve a jest,
Who knew that love could be such a fest?

Tiny scratches from playful hands,
Worn with time, just like old bands.
Once a vow, now a pun-filled rhyme,
Chasing echoes of a silly time.

With every glance, I see new glee,
A saga spun from pure esprit.
What once was serious, now a play,
A keeper of quirks, here to stay.

These carvings whisper, "Life's a game!"
Where hearts and laughter are the same.
Shake the dust off, give it a spin,
Hear the chuckles where love's always been.

Chasing the Light of Longing

Oh how I chase that beam so bright,
With dreams that tumble, left and right.
A flash of joy, then it's gone,
Like a cat's pursuit—what's wrong?

I grin at shadows, they dance and play,
In the corners of my heart, they stay.
Each twinkle whispers a comic tale,
Where love once sailed, now it's stale.

A glimmer of hope, a jest in the air,
I trip on memories without a care.
Chasing the spark like it's a race,
Stumbling over that cheeky space.

With every stumble, laughter near,
In this pursuit, I shed a tear.
For though it's silly, it feels just right,
Chasing those moments, heart's delight.

A Token's Tale of Endless Love

Once a bauble, lost in time,
Now it giggles with a silly rhyme.
This token tells of love absurd,
With every flutter, a silly word.

It's chased through scenes both bright and dim,
With echoes of laughter on a whim.
A tiny glimpse of what once was,
Now trips on laughs because it does!

An endless tale of twists and turns,
Where every moment, my spirit yearns.
Though often foolish, it charms so well,
With stories hidden, secrets to tell.

Through thick and thin, it barely brews,
And teases me with comical clues.
I hold it close, this trinket of fun,
In its wild tale, we're always one.

Enigma of the Heart's Treasure

In a box of bling and charms,

I found a trinket with strange alarms.

It giggled when I pulled the clasp,

And whispered secrets with a rasp.

A photo of someone in silly shoes,

Dancing wildly, singing blues.

It said, "Wear me, make a fuss!"

But I think it just wants a bus.

With every twist, a chuckle came,

This heart's treasure is quite the game.

It jests and plays, a merry tease,

In this odd jewel, I find my ease.

Each glance reveals a funny tale,

Where love and humor set the sail.

A heart's enigma, oh what a jest,

In this treasure, I feel so blessed!

Echoes from a Timeless Keep

From an old chest with a creaky hinge,

I found a memory that made me cringe.

It squeaked and squirmed, an awkward sight,

A wearable disco ball of delight.

Each echo held a jolly tune,

As if the past danced under the moon.

My hair now sparkles, a shiny fright,

I laugh and twirl in pure delight!

Old pictures, all crazy and bright,

Faces making silly poses, what a sight!

A time capsule of jest and cheer,

In this timeless keep, I shed a tear.

So here I wear this glowing find,

With joyful memories intertwined.

The echoes laugh with every sway,

Reminding me it's all okay!

Secrets Encased in Silver

A silver trinket tucked away,

Holds secrets from an ancient day.

It squeaks and leaks a funny lore,

Of love affairs and kitchen sore.

A heart it seems, with plans absurd,

Like telling jokes to the pet bird.

It puffs up tales of clumsy glee,

Of how grandma danced on a bumblebee!

Each revelation, a playful twist,

With laughter ringing through the mist.

In silver chains, these secrets lie,

Making me laugh until I cry.

So here I clasp this silly prize,

A treasure full of joyous surprise.

Its charms unravel in this song,

In this silver glow, I feel I belong!

The Keeper of Lost Moments

I met a keeper of lost delight,
In a quirky shop with twinkling light.
Items that giggle, jingle, and sway,
Each one telling tales of a funny day.

With socks that danced and hats that sang,
The keeper cracked jokes and joyously rang.
A spoon with a grin, a cup with a wink,
In every corner, more laughs to think.

Lost moments wrapped in a silly bow,
Like a pet goldfish that once said "hello."
Each artifact dripped with comical grace,
In this rich treasure of joy, I embrace.

So here I stand, with memories in hand,
The keeper of fun, as we both planned.
Together we laugh, in this whimsical place,
Where lost moments find their perfect space!

Ode to a Glimmering Past

Once shiny and bright, in a pocket it danced,
Where whispers of secrets and laughter pranced.
It held all the giggles of times gone awry,
In a world where the lost loves would often just fly.

A wobbly charm that clinks with delight,
It tells all the tales of its wild, breezy flights.
With a wink and a nudge, oh what fun it brings,
As memories twirl, on whimsical wings.

Through puddles of giggles, we chase after dreams,
In a universe filled with silly little schemes.
It knows all the moments, both silly and grand,
Each flicker, a witness, to life's merry band.

So here's to the past, let's dance and let's cheer,
With a sparkle and shine, we hold it so dear.
For laughter's a treasure, that we can't forget,
In a locket of joy, our hearts are all set.

Echoes of a Bated Breath

Beneath frilly skirts, it played hide and seek,
Fingers fumbling softly, feeling quite meek.
It held every crush that caused cheeky thrills,
Goodness, oh goodness, it's given us chills!

Each flick of the clasp sends shivers of cheer,
As echoes of giggles ring loud and clear.
It mirrors the sighs of a love-struck mistake,
When secrets were whispered and hearts had to quake.

Caught in sweet moments of accidental falls,
It chuckles at mishaps and silly love calls.
With every missed chance, it shares a sly grin,
In the game of romance, nobody's a win.

So as you hold me, remember the jest,
This charm may be silly, but life's truly blessed.
With laughter as currency, we'll trade and we'll play,
For echoes of laughter are here to stay!

The Hideaway of Lost Wishes

In corners of pockets, where dreams often nest,
It cradles the wishes we thought were the best.
From tiny nothings to wishes so grand,
Each twinkling delight, slips right through our hands.

Once lost in a fervor, those moments we crave,
They bubble with joy, like a jubilant wave.
With whimsical whispers, it giggles along,
As secrets slip out in a cheeky old song.

Like socks with no mates or bananas gone brown,
It knows all the riddles of life's silly clown.
The wishes may fade, yet they strain and persist,
In the hideaway, laughter forever exists.

So let's raise a toast to the dreams that we lost,
For in the realm of fun, there's never a cost.
With chuckles and chuckles, let our spirits fly,
In a world full of wishes, we'll never say bye!

Heartfelt Cradle of Memories

In this tiny treasure, a universe spins,
A cradle of stories where laughter begins.
From stumbles to giggles, it holds every tear,
Each memory dances, as moments draw near.

Wrapped up in mischief, it whispers of glee,
In wild jubilee, both you and me.
To chaos and fun, it raises a cheer,
As we dance through the past with nothing to fear.

It cradles our stories, both funny and bright,
With each little mishap, it holds us so tight.
In the tapestry woven with colorful threads,
We find that the laughter is what truly spreads.

So here's to the charm that makes us all grin,
Through every odd twist, it's where we begin.
In heartbeats of joy, let's craft memories bold,
In a cradle of laughter, may our tales be told.

A Window to Longing Eyes

A gleam caught my eye, what could it be?
A trinket of memories, or so I decree.
It dangles and swings, a curious sight,
Did it hide secrets, or just caught a light?

I grabbed it with glee, a tale to unfold,
Expecting romance, or maybe some gold.
Instead it held photos of pets long gone,
Wearing hats and sunglasses—who knew they'd con?

I chuckled aloud, what a wild ride!
Eyes that once sparkled now hid with pride.
It whispered of stories, both silly and sweet,
An heirloom of laughter, my heart skipped a beat.

So here it shall stay, my fun little find,
A window to joy, both heart and mind.
Each glance brings a smile, it's easy to see,
This treasure of laughter was meant just for me.

The Hidden Journey of Forgotten Keepsakes

In an old dusty box, I found something odd,
A trinket that shimmered, I gave it a nod.
It seemed to hold tales of laughter and cheer,
But first I must know, what's happened here?

Inside were some photos, a sock, and a spoon,
A rubber duck too, under the light of the moon.
Each glimmering piece hid a giggle or laugh,
As if they had come from a whimsical past.

The parrot was funny, it seemed quite alive,
Wearing a bowler and ready to jive.
Was it once dapper at some grand affair?
Or stuck in the attic without a care?

I chuckled again as I popped the lid shut,
The hidden journey had turned into a rut.
But oh what a joy, those keepsakes now found,
In memories laced, hilariously bound.

Between the Chains of Time

I found a small charm, lost in my room,
It jingled and jangled, declaring its doom.
What story it held, I simply can't guess,
Was it meant for romance, or just a hot mess?

Was it once on a necklace or perhaps on a key?
Looking at it closely, it beckoned to me.
I smiled at the thought, my imagination soared,
Could it be an amulet? Or rejected award?

Was it part of a crown, from a queen of dessert?
Or merely a button from an old, silly shirt?
Each twist and each turn opened portals of fun,
Beneath all that clutter, oh what had I won!

Between these chains lies a laughter divine,
An echo of memories, humorous design.
In a world full of treasure, joy holds the rhyme,
It's between these chains that I dance with time.

Heartbeats Encapsulated

A shiny odd thing, I felt quite amazed,
What heart did it capture, in moments it blazed?
With each little knock, my laughter awoke,
What memories swirled, in that quirky cloak?

Inside was a note, a love gone astray,
'You stole my last cookie, I've nothing to say!'
Yet somehow it tickled, my funny bone hinted,
This cherished forget-me-not had truly consented.

The heartbeats it held, quite silly and grand,
Blushing adventures, perhaps too well planned.
I chuckled and smiled, oh the joy they brought,
Our hearts encapsulated, who ever thought?

Now it sits proudly on my table of dreams,
A funny reminder of sweet, silly schemes.
In laughter and love, we all play our part,
These heartbeats in metal steal away my heart.

Whispers of a Hidden Heart

In a pocket so deep, quite snug and tight,
Lies a heart that whispers, oh what a sight!
With secrets and giggles, it came alive,
Tickling the moments, where laughter will thrive.

Once it was lost, in a coat from '09,
Found by a cat, who thought it divine!
It playfully purred, held memories sweet,
Turning each frown into light on its feet.

Late night confessions, with slumbering guests,
This jewel has seen all the very best quests.
From hilarious mishaps to love's funny dance,
It twinkles and winks, oh, what a romance!

So next time you peek where the lost things depart,
Remember the whispers of a hidden heart!
For laughter's the treasure that we often can't see,
In a space where its joy is forever set free.

Secrets Encased in Gold

Nestled in velvet, a tale of pure gold,
Secretive laughter from stories retold.
It's seen all the blunders, the sweet and the sour,
A witness to love, a giggly flower.

Oh, what a charm, with a mischievous grin,
Keeping all secrets, where should we begin?
From pranks with the frogs to dates that went sour,
It rolls on the floor, tossing petals of power.

One day, it was tossed in a tub full of fizz,
Popped up with a splash, oh, what a whizz!
It chuckled at bubbles, with glee that it spurted,
Leaving us laughing, our hearts surely flirted.

With memories encased that never grow old,
This little gold secret, so lively and bold,
Sprinkles of humor, in every detail,
An heirloom of laughter in life's playful tale.

Memories Carved in Time

In a world where the clock never takes a rest,
Memories dance, wearing humor as vest.
Carved in a timepiece, they tick and they chime,
Hilarious moments, all frozen in rhyme.

There's a joke from a friend, made in summer's glow,
A fruitcake on a birthday, oh how it did blow!
Frosting on faces, oh, how we did squeal,
This playful artifact lays joy at our heel.

Each tick is a chuckle, each tock is a grin,
Reminding us always to savor the spin.
With laughter in echoes, in times long gone by,
Memories carved, never let us pass by.

In the treasure of time, we gather and shine,
Threads of merriment intertwine, oh divine!
So keep those moments, let laughter bloom bright,
In a world that spins on, filled with joy and delight.

A Treasure of Forgotten Love

Hidden within, a treasure untold,
Whispers of love, from days long and bold.
With a wink to the past, it giggles with glee,
Tales of love lost, yet still a jubilee.

There are notes with some hearts, scribbled in haste,
Share tea with a ghost, don't let it go to waste!
With laughter like echoes from years that we jest,
Each treasure of love is a quirky little quest.

There's a sock on the floor, where it shouldn't be,
But love binds the mess, so joy is the key!
From mishaps to giggles, to hugs from afar,
This treasure holds secrets, just like a shooting star.

So lift that old lid, and let stories unfold,
A treasure of love, hilariously bold.
With laughter that twinkles in shadows we see,
Forgotten yet cherished, a sweet melody.

Love's Enchanted Timepiece

In a tiny frame, love's dance resides,
Ticking on whims, where laughter collides.
A clock that refuses to keep any time,
It laughs at the chaos, a partner in crime.

With each silly chime, old lovers arrive,
Wearing mismatched socks, just feeling alive.
They fumble and grin, each moment a tease,
Stumbling through time with the greatest of ease.

Oh, cherish the seconds that giggle and wink,
In this quirky realm, there's no need to think.
For the hands may be stuck, but the heart skips a beat,
In this merry old watch, life's humor's a treat.

So wind it with joy, let the stories unfold,
Of misadventured souls and laughter retold.
In this funny timepiece, the love never grows old,
Instead, it just twirls in its silver and gold.

The Archive of Distant Dreams

In a dusty old book with pages askew,
Reside tales of love where shenanigans brew.
Each dream comes alive with a humorous twist,
As the characters tumble, you can't help but jest.

Here's a knight in armor who forgot how to ride,
Chasing after dragons with a bumbling stride.
Or a princess who giggles, her crown all askew,
Sipping tea with trolls, what a peculiar crew!

So page after page, let the laughter unwind,
At the silly exploits of a whimsical kind.
For every old fable holds joy intertwined,
In this archive of dreams, pure fun you'll find.

So gather your friends, grab a plush little bear,
And dive into stories that dance in the air.
For the magic of laughter is always untamed,
In the archive of dreams, where joy is proclaimed.

A Glimmer Beneath the Surface

In a puddle of sunshine, the memories play,
With a splash and a giggle, they dance every day.
A glimmer of mischief that sparkles like dew,
Beneath the bright surface, there's fun waiting too.

A fish tells a joke with a flick of its tail,
While a frog in a top hat begins a grand tale.
Bubbles burst forth with laughter so loud,
As the world's little creatures gather around.

Oh, look! There's a snail with a hat and a cane,
Reciting sweet verses while dodging the rain.
In this whimsical pond, take a dip if you dare,
For the joy that awaits is beyond all compare.

So lift up your chin and embrace the delight,
In a splash of the warm sun, your heart will take flight.
For deep in the glimmer, the laughter is vast,
And the memories forged will forever last.

Pendant of Memories Unbound

With a swing and a twirl, a pendant does gleam,
Holding tales of old in its whimsical dream.
Each swirl tells a story, a giggly delight,
As it spins through the moments, both silly and bright.

A toaster once toasted a rave in the night,
And a kitchen mishap turned dinner to fright.
But each little mishap, each baking faux pas,
Became just a giggle, a grand old hurrah!

Oh, the memories spin as secrets take flight,
In a pendant that dances, oh what a sight!
So wear it with joy as the laughter goes on,
In this playful escape where the shadows are gone.

With each little glance, feel the laughter expand,
For in every memory, we let go of the bland.
So cherish the pendant, the humor unfound,
In the light of sweet memories, we are forever unbound.

A Treasure's Journey Through Time

In a drawer so deep, it lay,
A tiny trinket lost in dismay.
It giggled when the dust piled high,
Dreaming of days when it could fly.

Through pockets, bags, and coats it crept,
In busier nights where laughter leapt.
It twinkled with tales of frolic and cheer,
Whispering secrets, 'I'm still here!'

A photo inside, a grin wide and bright,
As it chuckled at love, a silly sight.
It held memories from parties grand,
Like the time someone lost pants at the band.

So treasure those moments, shine and gleam,
For laughter is gold in this silly dream.
The journey continues, not a stop in sight,
With a wink and a laugh, it dances in light.

The Silent Saga of Affection

In a box of bling, it sat quite still,
Shining with charm, oh what a thrill!
It listened to gossip with silent delight,
As lovers exchanged vows on a starry night.

With each twist and turn, tales did unfold,
Of kisses and hugs, stories retold.
It giggled a bit at the drama it saw,
From love letters penned to the ex that got raw.

The heart within danced to pop's sweet refrain,
While wondering why love was often in vain.
It just wanted to hug, hold tight, and cheer,
As hearts moved in sync with wine and a beer.

So here's to the tales, both silly and grand,
Of love in a trinket, and stars all unplanned.
This silent witness of laughter and loss,
Winks at the future while counting its gloss.

Heartbeats Within a Frame

Inside a tiny frame, a picture's a riot,
With faces so goofy, it's truly a diet!
Hearts beat in sync to a schadenfreude tune,
As they dance in the light of a pizza-themed moon.

It sees love's pranks, a clock that runs fast,
The moments they grinned, each silly blast.
A heart-shaped treasure, just like a dream,
With laughter-packed memories bursting the seam.

It watches the couples, their antics and glee,
As they poke fun at their odd jubilee.
Caught in a laugh, oh how time can fly,
A heartbeat captured, a wink in the eye.

So cherish each giggle, each joyous embrace,
For time's just a joker in this wild race.
With love's crazy laughter, all neatly contained,
The heart beats in rhythm, completely unchained.

The Pendant's Hidden Journey

Once a humble pendant, it wanted to roam,
Escaping the necklace, it planned a grand home.
It slipped off one night with a cheeky desire,
To dance with the stars, oh, it could aspire!

It traveled to parties, where all were a blur,
Winking at crushes, creating a stir.
It laughed at the antics, a playful delight,
As it twirled with the music, oh what a sight!

Each twist in the air, it felt so alive,
A tiny explorer, with sass to survive.
It shared in the whispers of secrets and dreams,
Chasing down wishes like sunbeams and streams.

So here's to adventures, each jig and each jive,
For laughter's a gemstone that keeps us alive.
With love in its heart, this pendant will shine,
In a world full of humor, where joy's in the line.

Unwritten Tales of Affection

In a box of odds and ends,
A trinket hid from view,
It laughed at all the secrets,
Of love it never knew.

It jiggled in a pocket,
As I dashed to catch my train,
Like a squirrel in a circus,
It danced through joy and pain.

With every twist and tumble,
It tried to make a plan,
To find a match, a spark,
Or a proper, handsome man.

But alas! It squished a sandwich,
And got jammed with my keys,
Its dreams of romance faltered,
As it clung to crumbs with ease.

The Forgotten Token's Journey

Once a keychain of wonders,
Now it's lost its charm,
With pizza stains and laughter,
It's outgrown its former calm.

It's seen the bottom of bags,
And dined on lint and crumbs,
While scheming grand adventures,
With squirrels and ransacked drums.

From fidget spinners to paperclips,
It tells of wild exploits,
Though now it mostly watches,
As I lose my socks and hoist.

So here it sits a relic,
In a drawer full of dreams,
With a grin that's ever lazy,
While the world is more than it seems.

Whispers of Forgotten Memories

In the attic dust and shadows,
A bauble took a ride,
Through boxes full of giggles,
And old secrets to hide.

It remembered all the stories,
Of blunders and of fun,
Like the time it dropped a cake,
And everyone did run.

With a twinkle and a nudge,
It tried to break the norm,
But got stuck out of laughter,
And fell into the swarm.

Now it chuckles in the silence,
With memories that delight,
For each stumble is a treasure,
That makes the heart feel light.

Heartstrings Woven in Gold

A shiny bit of laughter,
It jigs with every beat,
Worn on days of sunshine,
And evenings bittersweet.

It hops between the moments,
With every crazy dance,
Trying to match the rhythm,
Of a never-ending chance.

Though it may seem forgotten,
In the midst of life's great race,
It twinkles with a purpose,
To keep a smiling face.

And in the end it whispers,
In a voice that's slightly grand,
Life's a tapestry of giggles,
Woven by our hand.

The Glow of Distant Remembrance

Once I found a tiny charm,
Thought it would bring me great balm.
But every glance made me frown,
It always tumbled right down.

I put it in my pocket tight,
Hoping it could bring delight.
Instead, it danced with my keys,
Oh, how it laughed at my pleas!

I tried to make it a crown,
But it just rolled back down.
A playful little old friend,
I guess it's better to pretend.

Now it glows with stories old,
Of jumbles and laughter untold.
I treasure each silly chat,
That charm's a real acrobat!

Celestial Chimes from Yesterday

In the drawer lay a trinket,
Next to coins and an old ticket.
I shook it, heard a silly jingle,
Made me laugh and then just mingle.

Once it glimmered at a dance,
Wearing it gave me a chance.
But as I twirled with glee and flair,
It slipped away, oh what a scare!

By the cat it did cling tight,
A snatch and dash, what a fright!
That feline thought it was a toy,
Adding more chaos, oh what joy!

Now it chimes a silly tune,
Underneath the laughing moon.
I hold it dear, this quirky piece,
A joyful laugh that brings me peace.

Whispers Encased in Adornments

In a box of shiny things,
I found a clip with dragon wings.
It whispered tales of days gone by,
While I just giggled at the sky.

It tried to take me on a ride,
But it just flopped and slid aside.
With every twist, it made a fuss,
I couldn't help but laugh with trust.

It once was worn by a queen so bold,
Now it's just a story retold.
Its sparkles shine in shadows faint,
As mischievous as a little saint.

So here I keep my winged delight,
In a world of laughter and light.
A friendship forged with every joke,
Bound in whispers and a little smoke.

Time's Talisman of Affection

A curious thing, a button bright,
It claims to hold love's purest light.
But in my drawer, it does reside,
Laughing at all that I've applied.

Tried to wear it on a date,
But it jumped and sealed my fate.
Rolling under tables, oh dear,
What a scene, the end was near!

I found it stuck in my hair,
The date just couldn't help but stare.
A wild twist, a comical plight,
Love's journey led to that sight.

Now it sits with pride and cheer,
Each time I see it, brings good beer.
A talisman of memory and play,
In the light of each silly day!

www.ingramcontent.com/pod-product-compliance
Lightning Source LLC
Chambersburg PA
CBHW070322120526
44590CB00017B/2787